中區警署建築群

·

謝 幕

CURTAIN CALL

·

The Central Police Station Compound

中區警署建築群

·

謝 幕

CURTAIN CALL

·

The Central Police Station Compound

梁家泰 LEONG KA TAI

OXFORD

UNIVERSITY PRESS

OXFORD
UNIVERSITY PRESS

Oxford University Press is a department of the University of Oxford.
It furthers the University's objective of excellence in research, scholarship,
and education by publishing worldwide. Oxford is a registered trade mark of
Oxford University Press in the UK and in certain other countries

Published in Hong Kong by
Oxford University Press (China) Limited
39th Floor, One Kowloon, 1 Wang Yuen Street, Kowloon Bay, Hong Kong

中區警署建築群
·
謝 幕

CURTAIN CALL
·
The Central Police Station Compound

梁家泰 LEONG KA TAI

ISBN: 978-0-19-398846-0

Impression: I

目錄 TABLE OF CONTENTS

中區警署建築群
HISTORIC BUILDINGS OF
THE CENTRAL POLICE STATION COMPOUND

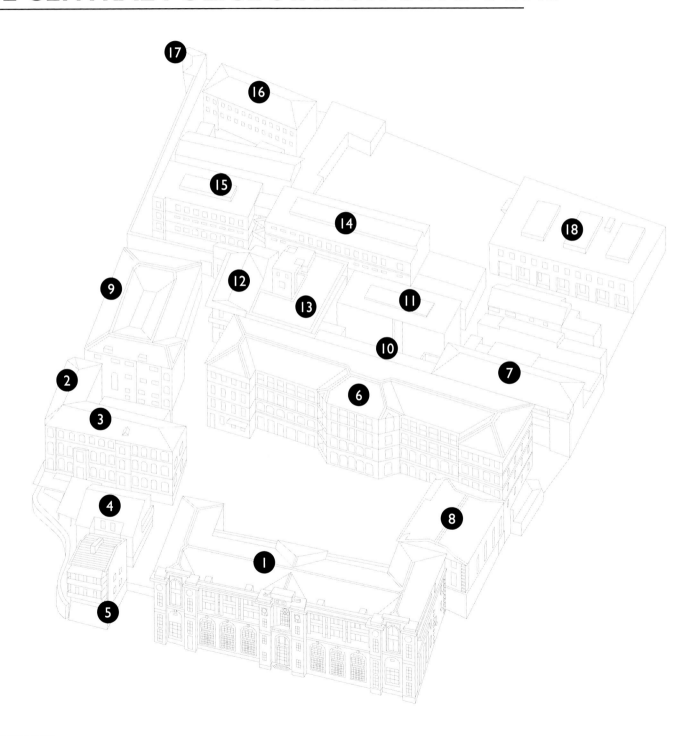

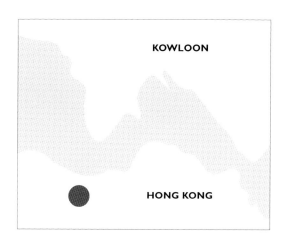

1 總部大樓　**Headquarters Block**

2 A座　**Block A**

3 B座　**Block B**

4 C座　**Block C**

5 D座　**Block D**

6 營房大樓　**Barrack Block**

7 衛生樓　**Sanitary Block**

8 馬廄　**Stable Block**

9 中央裁判司署　**Central Magistracy**

10 A倉　**A Hall**

11 B倉　**B Hall**

12 C倉（東翼）　**C Hall (East Wing)**

13 C倉（西翼）　**C Hall (West Wing)**

14 D倉（西翼）　**D Hall (West Wing)**

15 D倉（東翼）　**D Hall (East Wing)**

16 E倉　**E Hall**

17 更樓（紫荊樓）　**Watch Tower (Bauhinia House)**

18 F倉　**F Hall**

歷史時間表 HISTORICAL TIMELINE

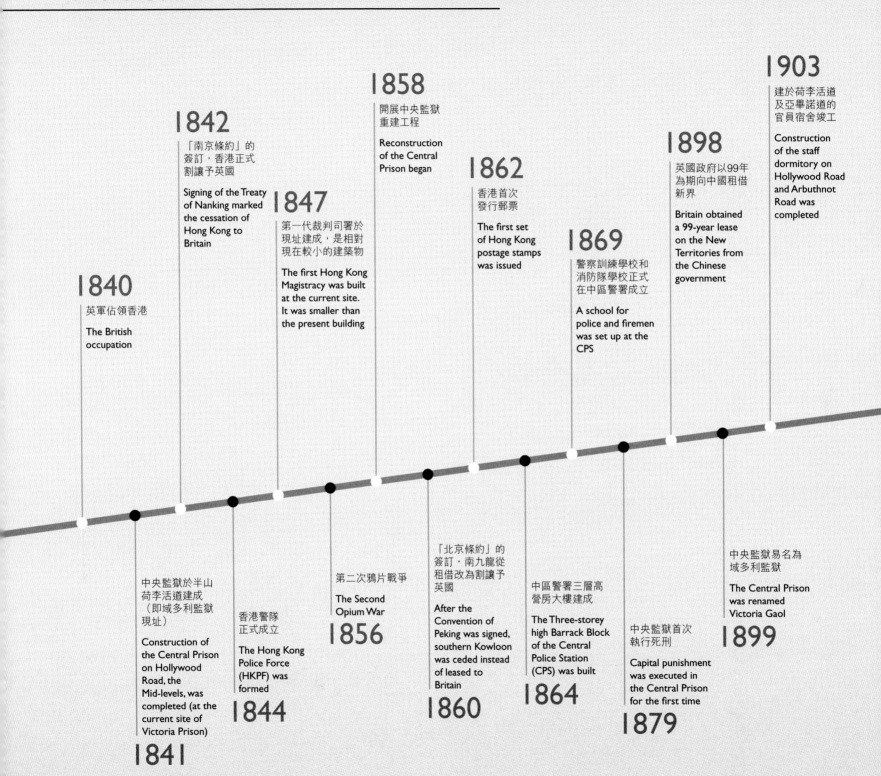

1840

英軍佔領香港

The British occupation

1841

中央監獄於半山荷李活道建成（即域多利監獄現址）

Construction of the Central Prison on Hollywood Road, the Mid-levels, was completed (at the current site of Victoria Prison)

1842

「南京條約」的簽訂，香港正式割讓予英國

Signing of the Treaty of Nanking marked the cessation of Hong Kong to Britain

1844

香港警隊正式成立

The Hong Kong Police Force (HKPF) was formed

1847

第一代裁判司署於現址建成，是相對現在較小的建築物

The first Hong Kong Magistracy was built at the current site. It was smaller than the present building

1856

第二次鴉片戰爭

The Second Opium War

1858

開展中央監獄重建工程

Reconstruction of the Central Prison began

1860

「北京條約」的簽訂，南九龍從租借改為割讓予英國

After the Convention of Peking was signed, southern Kowloon was ceded instead of leased to Britain

1862

香港首次發行郵票

The first set of Hong Kong postage stamps was issued

1864

中區警署三層高營房大樓建成

The Three-storey high Barrack Block of the Central Police Station (CPS) was built

1869

警察訓練學校和消防隊學校正式在中區警署成立

A school for police and firemen was set up at the CPS

1879

中央監獄首次執行死刑

Capital punishment was executed in the Central Prison for the first time

1898

英國政府以99年為期向中國租借新界

Britain obtained a 99-year lease on the New Territories from the Chinese government

1899

中央監獄易名為域多利監獄

The Central Prison was renamed Victoria Gaol

1903

建於荷李活道及亞畢諾道的官員宿舍竣工

Construction of the staff dormitory on Hollywood Road and Arbuthnot Road was completed

1906
中區警署營房
大樓加建一層

A storey was
added to the
Barrack Block of
the CPS

1914
新裁判司署於
原址落成，定名
為中央裁判司署，
同年警隊成立
交通部

A new magistracy,
named the Central
Magistracy, was
built at the original
site. The HKPF
established the
traffic division

1919
中區警署總部
大樓落成

The headquarters
of the CPS was
built

1925
中區警署成立
攝影部

A photography
division was set
up at the CPS

1928
啟德機場
正式啟用

Kai Tak Airport
began operation

1936
警隊正式招募
第一批華籍督察

The HKPF
recruited the
first batch of
Chinese
sub-inspectors

1938
中央裁判司署
頂層進行大規模
改建，監獄署正
式成立

The top floor
of the Central
Magistracy
underwent
major alterations.
The Prisons
Department was
founded

1941
日軍佔領香港，
裁判司署被用作
審判戰爭罪犯的
特別法庭，域多利
收押所用以囚禁
英軍，中區警署則
用作日軍警察總部

During the Japanese
occupation, the
Japanese used the
Central Magistracy
as a special court to
try war criminals,
Victoria Remand
Prison to imprison
British soldiers and
the CPS as their
police headquarters

1912
第一代裁判司署
完全清拆

Demolition of the
first Magistracy

1915
中央裁判司署首次
用作司法審理

The first case was
tried at the Central
Magistracy

1923
刑事偵緝部在
中區警署成立

The Criminal
Investigation
Department as
founded at the CPS

1927
後備警隊（即現時
的輔警）成立

The Hong Kong
Police Reserve
(now the Hong
Kong Auxiliary
Police Force) was
established

1931
油麻地警署供奉
警隊第一座的
關帝像

The Yau Ma Tei
Police Station was
the first in the
HKPF to enshrine
the statue of
Guangung

1937
時稱香港監獄的
赤柱監獄開始
運作，死刑亦改在
那裏執行，域多利
監獄關閉，同年
中日戰爭爆發

After the opening
of the Hong Kong
Prison (now Stanley
Prison), Victoria
Gaol was closed
down and execution
of the death penalty
was moved to the
new site. The
Sino-Japanese War
broke out

1939
域多利監獄易名為
域多利收押所，
拘留等後審訊的
犯人

Victoria Gaol was
renamed Victoria
Remand Prison
to hold offenders in
custody prior
to trials

1945
日本戰敗，英國再度接管香港

After the surrender of Japan, Britain regained control over Hong Kong

1953
實施「犯人工資計劃」

The Prisons Department introduced the Earnings Scheme

銅鑼灣填海計劃完成

Land reclamation in Causeway Bay was completed

1960
精神病觀察中心在域多利收押所成立處理及治療有精神及情緒問題的犯人

The Psychiatric Observation Unit was set up at the Victoria Remand Prison to handle and treat prisoners with mental and/or psychological illnesses

1966
最後一次死刑在赤柱執行

The last death penalty was carried out in Stanley Prison

1968
警察機動部隊成立

The Police Tactical Unit was set up

1972
紅磡海底隧道啟用通車

The Cross-Harbour Tunnel opened for traffic

小欖精神病院啟用，同時開始接收有精神問題的犯人

Siu Lam Psychiatric Centre came into operation and began to accommodate prisoners with mental health problems

1977
荔枝角收押所啟用，域多利收押所改名為域多利監獄

Lai Chi Kok Reception Centre was opened. Victoria Reception Centre was renamed Victoria Prison

1980
取消抵壘政策對中國內地的非法入境者採取即捕即解政策

The Touch Base Policy was abolished. Illegal immigrants intercepted were to be repatriated immediately

興建香港第一個廉租屋邨北角模範邨

Construction of North Point Model Housing Estate, the first low-cost housing estate in Hong Kong

1951

警察總部遷到灣仔軍器廠街

The Police Headquarters relocated to Arsenal Street

1954

香港出現嚴重的水荒，規定每天供水4小時，及後出現每4天供水一次，每次4小時

Serious drought affected Hong Kong. Water was rationed for 4 hours each day, and later further reduced to 4 hours every 4 days

1963

香港暴動，域多利收押所易名域多利羈留中心

During the 1967 riots, Victoria Remand Prison was changed to Victoria Reception Centre

1967

香港正式訂立婚姻「一夫一妻」制

Monogamous marriage was institutionalized

英女王御賜「皇家」予香港警隊，從此改名「皇家香港警察」

Queen Elizabeth II granted the "Royal" prefix to the HKPF, renaming it the Royal Hong Kong Police Force

1969

廉政專員公署成立

The Independent Commission Against Corruption was established

中文成為法定語言

Chinese was made Hong Kong's second official language

1974

中央裁判司署關閉裁判司署遷出建築物。香港正式成為難民「第一收容港」

The Central Magistracy was decommissioned, and the Magistracy moved out. Hong Kong declared itself the "port of first asylum"

1979

1982

監獄署正式易名
為懲教署

The Prisons
Department was
renamed the
Correctional
Services
Department

1988

65名「無證媽媽」
被遣返，由報到至
遣返的過程均在
中區警署及域多利
監獄進行

A group of 65
mothers staying
illegally in Hong Kong
were repatriated.
The whole process
was carried out at
the Central Prison
and Victoria Prison

1992

司法部改稱為
香港司法部機構

The Judiciary
of Hong Kong
changed its name
in Chinese

1997

香港回歸中國
警隊亦隨之改名
為「香港警察」

The "Royal Hong
Kong Police Force"
was renamed
the "Hong Kong
Police Force" upon
the handover of
sovereignty of
Hong Kong to
China

2003

嚴重急性呼吸系統
綜合症（沙士）在
香港爆發

Outbreak of Severe
Acute Respiratory
Syndrome (SARS)

2006

域多利監獄
停止運作

Closing of the
Victoria Prison

2010

香港國際攝影節
在中區警署舉行
開幕典禮及
《香港最早期
照片攝影展》

The Hong Kong
International
Photo Festival
held its opening
ceremony and the
"First Photographs
of Hong Kong"
exhibition
at the CPS

政府接納馬會
活化建築群的
修訂方案

The Government
accepted the
HKJC's revised
design for the
revitalization
project of the CPS

香港聯合聲明
正式生效

Sino-British Joint
Declaration came
into effect

1985

《香港基本法》
正式頒佈

The Basic Law was
promulgated

1990

古物古蹟辦事處列
中區警署、中央
裁判司署及域多利
監獄為法定古蹟

The Antiquities and
Monuments Office
declared the CPS,
Central Magistracy
and Victoria Prison
as monuments in
Hong Kong

1995

啟德機場關閉，取而
代之的是赤鱲角的
香港國際機場

Kai Tak Airport was
closed and replaced
by the Hong Kong
International Airport
at Chek Lap Kok

1998

警隊正式將中區
警署交回政府

Closing of the CPS

2005

施政報告宣佈原則
上接受香港賽馬會
的活化計劃，項目
預算耗資18億元

According to the
Policy Address, the
CPS Revitalisation
Project proposed by
The Hong Kong
Jockey Club (HKJC)
was accepted in
principle and was
estimated to cost
$1.8 billion

2007

序

香港第一所監獄正式來説其實只是一間棚屋，到了1862年，一所較正規的監獄建成，這就是後來的域多利監獄D座。在其一旁的中區警署於1864年建成，而中央裁判司署則在1914年完工。可以説，這三座建築物構成了香港的「執法鐵三角」，拘捕，審訊及監禁罪犯全在同一個地方進行。及後，因着不斷膨脹的人口，為了更有效運用空間，陸續在香港其他地區建立新址，裁判司署首先於1979年遷出，中區警署於2004年關閉，最後域多利監獄於2006年停止運作。

但是歷史和年份並不是這影集的重點。

中區警署建築群停用後，我有幸獲古物古蹟辦事處批准，進入建築物內拍攝照片。於是，在2006年11月至12月間的這五個星期裏，我每天帶着一台大片幅相機（那種你需要把頭埋在黑布下才可看見影像的老古董），走遍建築群每個樓層角落，尋找最堪人回味的拍攝角度。

熟悉攝影的人會明白，這不是一件易事。當年建築群可能是附近地區內最高的建築物，但在我拍攝的時候，建築群已被同區其他高樓大廈所包圍。每天，只有數分鐘的時間能在建築群內見到從大廈樓縫間溜進來的陽光。幸而有現代建築幕牆的出現，遠至西區街市的大廈，也能把多一點點的陽光反射到建築群裏。於是，時機成了一切的關鍵。使用大片幅相機，每次拍攝前也需幾分鐘預備，這意味着要預測陽光的走向，而要有準確的預測，又得花上好幾天去觀察，以了解陽光在建築群內的軌跡。例如，你需要在

11:14分做好準備，捕捉從總部大樓正門溜進來的陽光；到了13:32分，目標就換成是陽光從雲咸街立健商業大廈反射到警署B座陽台形成光影交錯的景象；又或是在16:25分拍攝由招商局集團大廈反映到營房大樓房間的陽光。如果遇上突然飄過的雲朵，遮擋了光線，一番部署就打空了。建築群內光線普遍偏暗，而為了保存地方的氛圍，照片得要以自然光線拍攝。加上慢速菲林（ISO50）和收細了的鏡頭光圈，曝光時間便偏長了。有一次，曝光長達一小時，那我就利用了那段時間來尋找下一個拍攝位置。

至於喜歡歷史的人，本書記錄這座在1841年香港割讓予英國後隨即興建的古蹟。這個歷史場地已不復存在，不單是建築群已作全面的翻新工程，加入新的（有些人説是格格不入的）建築，而部份B座又於翻新期間倒塌。其實，建築物早已殘破非常，我在拍攝期間也得極度小心。現在回想，幸好我冒着危險，爬上那些搖搖欲墜的樓梯，留下的照片現已無法重拍了。

場地有其歷史價值，建築也別具一格，但我的興趣卻不盡在此兩處。我不只是要記錄當下的實況，同時希望喚起昔日的感覺 —— 囚犯度過日以繼夜的監房、不幸在獄中過身囚犯的殮息處、非法入境者的孩子們玩耍的空間、絕望時成為勉慰的牆上塗鴉；我還想展示總部大樓和營房大樓的一般日常，警務員執勤時如何與環境互動，裁判司又是如何運作。

這就是為甚麼在拍攝建築群的五個星期過去後，我決定為

照片補充相關的解説。原來這比拍攝照片困難得多！

我決定找一些與建築群有關的人士，包括警員，懲教人員，守衛員，甚至釋囚分享他們在建築群時的生活和一些有趣的故事，還有他們對這地方的回憶。相信任何曾參與口述歷史相關工作的人都可以告訴你，低估當中的工作量是一件近乎必然發生的事。

我幸得朋友幫忙，給我介紹退休警務人員和懲教人員，我甚至找來一名（似乎非常享受牢獄生涯的）前囚犯，至於曾在那裏工作的法官，在我着手這計劃時，年紀大都相當老邁，因此一直無法找到一位作訪問對象。

我挑選了一輯照片，然後向我訪問的對象逐張展示，以勾起他們對照片的反應。這書不是要複述既有歷史，因此我鼓勵他們說出個人感受。在某方面，我是頗成功的。透過這些訪問，我得知了某位警員前往面試時經過總部大樓每道門時的感受，也聽到了一些鬼故事，耳聞了駐診醫生治病獨特的方法，了解到在槍房工作有多沉悶與高壓，但又感受到那份獲上級信任的光榮。我又聽到懲教人員在監獄空地，囚犯虎視眈眈下，排隊領取現金薪酬時的感受；聽到一個經常到獄中探望越南船民的神父感歎獄中石地的冰冷……所有所有的這些也讓我窺見建築物裏曾有過的不同生活。

可是把這些資料梳理成一個連貫的整體又成為另一項幾乎無法完成的工作。建築群與人事多年間不停變化，每個

地方也因時因事而有不同的運用，在訪問當中，常會出現一位訪問者堅持某地方作某種用途而另一人卻又堅持別的。舉例，一位警員不斷強調在總部大樓東翼一樓常常會聞到燒羊架的香味，因為那裏是警官食堂；但另一警員又説那裏除了辦公室外，就沒有其他了。另一例是，當所有人也説大地旁的芒果樹結果那年，必會有壞事發生（例如1967），有人喜歡吃這些芒果，而有人卻説味道又苦又澀。或許有經驗的口述歷史工作者總找到方法協調平凡細節當中小矛盾，但我卻苦無頭緒。

當我試圖去整理和驗證這些解説時，計劃就這樣停滯不前，轉眼幾年又過去。

後來，我突然意識到原來自己誤入歧途。回到初衷，這本書從不是關於歷史，而是人與建築物間的互動，在監房的感受，看管囚犯時的感受，執法時的感受，在法庭中伸張正義的感受。這些解説無疑是個人的，是趣聞，是回憶，是軼事，雖然不能通過嚴格的學術評審，但他們代表了一種主觀的視點。而這視點不是指向可驗證的解説，而是要讓人眼前一亮，為讀者提供更多有關照片的背景資料。

就這樣，經數年的反覆推敲，這本書才終告完成。我希望讀者會欣賞照片，也能藉文字對中區警署建築群往日的生活有多一份的了解。這場地已用嶄新的模式現世了。

梁家泰

INTRODUCTION

The first prison built in Hong Kong was a shed, but a proper prison was built in 1862. It was later named D-Block of Victoria Prison. The Police Station was then built in 1864 next to it, and after that, the Magistrates' Court in 1914. Together they formed what I would call the "Law Enforcement Triangle", where perpetrators would be arrested, tried and incarcerated all in one place. But as the facilities could not keep up with the population, new sites in Hong Kong were set up for more efficient use of space. The Magistrates' Court was the first to move in 1979, the Police Headquarters in 2004, and finally, Victoria Prison in 2006.

This book, however, is not about historical facts and dates.

Soon after the whole Compound was decommissioned, I was fortunate enough to obtain permission, from the Antiquities and Monuments Office, to photograph the buildings. For five weeks in November and December 2006, I went there every day, with a view camera (the kind where you have to hide under a cloth to see the image), exploring every nook and cranny, looking for interesting angles to photograph.

Those interested in photography would see right away that this was not an easy task. The Compound comprised probably the highest buildings in the area when it was built, but at the time when I was taking photographs, it was surrounded by high-rise buildings. Sunlight could only sneak in through gaps between the buildings for a few minutes before it was blocked again, and thanks to modern curtain wall construction, sunlight was also reflected into the rooms from buildings as far away as the Western Market area. Timing was key. With the view camera, which always requires a few minutes to set up, it meant anticipating where the sun would be, setting up, and waiting for the light to arrive. It took quite a few days' observation to get to know the sun's trajectory among the buildings and it could be frustrating if a cloud suddenly decided to wander in and block the light. One had to be ready at 11:14 to catch the sunlight streaming in through the front door of the Police Headquarters Building, at 13:32 for the sunlight reflected off the Vogue Building on neighbouring Wyndham Street to create patterns of light and shadows on the balcony of Block B at

the Police Station or 16:25 to photograph sun rays reflected off the China Merchants Group Building shining into a room in the Barrack Block. Even then, the amount of light in the buildings was in general very low – the photographs had to be taken with any available natural light, to preserve the ambiance of the location. With slow film (exposed at ISO50) and a small lens aperture, this called for rather long exposures. In one case, I had to set the exposure for an hour (I took the time to wander around looking for the next angle).

And for those interested in history, this book can be seen as documentation of a heritage site, construction of which started just a few years after 1841, when Hong Kong was ceded to the British. The historical site, as it was, exists no more. Not only has the Compound now been renovated completely, with new, (some would consider rather incongruous) buildings added, two of the original buildings, Block B of the Police Compound, partially collapsed during renovation. I have to say that these buildings were considered dangerously weak and I had to take great care not to step on the wrong places when taking photographs there. But it was fortunate that I decided to risk my neck and my limbs to climb up those rickety stairs. These images cannot be taken again.

The buildings certainly have historical value and their architecture is still fascinating, but my interest went beyond that. My aim was not just to document the physical state of the Compound, but to evoke the feeling of the Compound when it was occupied – the cells where the prisoners spent their days and nights, and where the unfortunate few were laid to rest, the little play area for the offspring of illegal immigrants, graffiti on the wall as consolation at times of despair; and I also wanted to show what life was like at the Police Station, the HQ Block and the Barrack Block, how the police personnel interacted with their environment as they carried out their duties, and how the Magistrates' Court worked.

That was why, after the five weeks photographing the Compound, I decided to supplement the content of the photographs with related commentary. It turned out to be even more difficult than the photography!

What I wanted to do was to find people who were connected with the Compound – policemen, correctional service officers, custodians and, yes, even prisoners, to give me accounts of life in the Compound. I would interview them, and they would tell me, with their interesting stories, what they remembered about the places. As anybody who has done any work with oral history will tell you, it is really easy to underestimate the work involved.

I was fortunate in that I received help from friends. They introduced me to retired policemen and correctional service officers. We had quite a few good chats. I even found a former convict (who seemed to enjoy his incarceration immensely). It was impossible to find a magistrate. Those who worked there were much too old by the time I started this project.

My methodology was to make a set of prints of selected images I had taken and show them one by one to the interviewees, to elicit their responses to the prints. I encouraged them to be as personal as possible, since the purpose of the book was not to regurgitate official history. In a way, I was quite successful. I was told of how a certain constable felt when she walked through the doors of the Headquarters Building on the way to her job review. I was told ghost stories. I was told of the idiosyncratic ways the doctor treated the sick. I was told of how boring, and under how much pressure, being on duty in the gun room could be — but it was a sign of trust from the superiors, so it was an honour. I was told of how the correctional officers felt to be lined up in the prison courtyard to be paid, in cash, under the eyes of the convicts lounging around. I was told, by a priest, who visited the Vietnamese boat people held there, how he felt the cold of the stones in the prison. All these comments have given me insights into life in the Compound from different perspectives.

But to incorporate all these different perspectives into a coherent whole turned out to be an almost impossible task. The buildings and personnel had gone through many changes during the years. The rooms were used for different purposes as time and circumstances changed. So it became quite common that one interviewee would insist that the location shown in one image was used for one purpose while another interviewee would contradict that with equal insistence. For example, one police officer said that the east wing of the first floor of the HQ Block smelled of lamb chops when he was there, since it housed the officers' mess, but another officer would insist that it had always been used as offices and nothing more. As another example, while everybody agreed that the mango tree bearing fruit in the courtyard of the police compound was an omen of impending disaster (citing the 1967 riots), some would say that the fruits were bitter and dry but some would savour the taste of the mangoes. Trivial details, perhaps, and for an experienced practitioner in oral history, there would surely be numerous ways to reconcile the inconsistencies, but somehow I could not find my way through them.

Thus it was that the project dragged on for years, while I tried to collate and verify the comments.

However, I have now come to the realisation that I have been sidetracked – from the very start, this book is not about historical facts, but the interaction between the buildings and the people occupying them – how it felt to be confined in the cells, to watch over the prisoners, to perform one's duties in the name of the law, and to mete out justice in the courts. The comments are certainly personal and anecdotal, and perhaps may not be admissible under strict academic scrutiny, but they represent a subjective point of view. The point is thus not of verifying the comments, but of choosing those that are the most enlightening, those that give the reader the most insight into the background of the photographs.

So now, after years of consideration, we have finally this book. I hope that the reader will enjoy the photographs and gain insights into life in the former Central Police Station Compound, which exists now in a completely new form.

Leong Ka Tai

中區警署

CENTRAL POLICE STATION

總部大樓

又稱紅屋，相中所見大樓前的空地亦有其別稱，來得有氣勢，且具詩意，叫「大地」。1967年前，大地平日泊滿私家車，能佔一席位，最少也得是幫辦級（督察）；「六七暴動」後，大地就只予停泊防暴警察及機動部隊的車輛。

相中芒果樹據說快有一百歲，常年不開花結果。若那年花兒盛開又果實纍纍，多有不妙之大事發生。這是警隊中人所共知的，故沒人願見其花果。在資料搜集過程中訪問的多位警員也憶及1967那年，果實特別豐盛。

總部大樓關閉當天，大地舉行了鳴金收兵禮，代表這建築物正式告別其歷史使命，聽說很多在場的警員也灑下了男兒淚。

Headquarters Block

Also known as the Red House or the Big Station, the Headquarters Block stood in front of the Parade Ground. The latter, open and majestic, was dearly called as daai dei in Cantonese, which literally meant "the grand earth". It was used for parking and was often packed with private cars belonging to officers holding the rank of or above Inspector of Police. After the 1967 Riots, however, it became exclusive to the Anti-riot Squad and the Tactical Unit.

The mango tree in the foreground is rumoured to be 100 years old, and that though it rarely flowers or bears fruit; when it does, calamity strikes, so that no one wished to see it happens. Many of the policemen interviewed in this project would recall the exquisite blooms in 1967.

On the decommissioning day of the Headquarters Block, a ceremony of Beating Retreat was held to mark the end of the building's historical mission. Many were said to have shed tears.

總部大樓正門

樓層從荷李活道起算，所以這是三樓。

「那時到紅屋進行升職面試，一進門，上了蠟的地板光亮如鏡，差不多可照見你每顆牙齒。我邊走邊抖，心慌意亂，腦袋一片空白。曾聽說有警員因太緊張，面試時暈倒。」一位警員憶述他踏進這大門的經歷。

總部大樓是高級警務人員辦公室，也設有俱樂部。除了呈送文書或接受升職面試，一般警員甚少內進。1952年灣仔警察總部建成前，香港警務署處長辦公室就設在這大樓裏。

Main Entrance, Headquarters Block

Starting from the Hollywood Road level as the ground floor, this is the second floor.

"I went to the Red House for a promotion interview. The waxed floor inside the main entrance shone like a mirror. You could almost see every tooth in your mouth. I shook as I walked on it. My heart trembled and my mind went blank. I heard some officer was so nervous that he fainted at an interview," an officer recalled his experience walking through the Main Entrance.

The Headquarters Block housed the offices of the senior officers as well as a club. Lower-ranking officers rarely came here save for dispatch of documents and promotion interviews. It was also the office of the Commissioner of Police before the new headquarters in Wanchai was built in 1952.

總部大樓正門樓梯

往上是高級警員餐廳，只供警司、總督察以上職級內進；
向下是通往交通部。

照片中陽光如煦灑落於階梯間，但當時一般警員不太樂於
在這樓梯上落。原因是，往上走大多會碰見上級，得不停
打招呼，前一句 Morning Sir，後一句 Morning Sir 般，很
是煩人；往下到交通部大多有撞車或其他交通事故，感覺
不吉利。

Staircase near the Main Entrance, Headquarters Block

The staircase led up to the dining room for Chief Inspectors of
Police, Superintendents of Police or any senior-ranking officers,
and down to the Traffic Division.

Though the staircase in the photograph was lit by warm sunshine,
most officers did not enjoy using it. Going up, one would very
likely run into senior officers and be awkwardly repeating
"Morning, Sir"; while going down to the Accident Investigation
Section is considered inauspicious.

東側門樓梯

通往便衣探員（CID）辦公室房，再往裏走是中區分房。

樓上探員工作的房間有大細房之分，大房有一張大長枱，最多可讓十多名警員同時向疑犯錄取口供。警隊習慣在便衣探員辦公大房供奉關公。而細房會作盤問疑犯之用，房頂設有隔音天花，天花上有一層鐵籠，以防犯人逃走。

Staircase, East End Entrance, Headquarters Block

This staircase led to the CID office and further to the central common room.

The CID office comprised a large and a small room. The large room contained a long bench where about a dozen of detectives could take statements from suspects simultaneously. There is also a statue of Guangong (Deity of Loyalty and Justice) in the large room. The small room, where the roof was sound-proof and reinforced with a grille to prevent suspects from escaping, was used for interrogation.

總部大樓四樓陽台

照片中由露台往外看到的，是警署在對面大廈玻璃幕牆上的倒影，但過去看到的則是一座座相距甚近的舊樓建築。再往外走，是附近的奧卑利街和石板街，那裏曾有排擋，賣古董、地毯的店舖，而荷李活道及擺花街上有打鐵的、賣生果的、還有剪髮店。1960年代，石板街上有一間「榮記」的細小士多，很多警員也常去光顧。

當時很多市民也不習慣與警員在同一間餐室中一起用餐，因此若警員要休息喝茶用點，會去指定的餐廳。這些餐廳事前作了查詢，確定了店主不介意警察入內用餐小休。

Third Floor Veranda, Headquarters Block

Looking out from the veranda nowadays, one sees the reflection of the Headquarters Block on the glass curtain wall of the opposite building. In the past, one would see blocks of old buildings set in close proximity. There were pai dongs (open-air food stalls), antique and rug shops nearby on Old Bailey Street and Pottinger Street, as well as blacksmiths, fruit vendors and barbers on Hollywood Road and Lyndhurst Terrace. In the 1960s, a small kiosk on Pottinger Street called Wing Kee (榮記) was popular with the police.

Local people felt uneasy sharing an eatery with police officers. Therefore, the officers would only go to designated ones that welcomed them.

總部大樓四樓陽台

相中通道，曾經擺放了滿滿的鋼製文件櫃，聞說文職人員在上班前又或是中午會在此耍太極健身。

照片的視點是警官俱樂部外望，另一邊盡頭的圓窗後是便衣探員（CID）的辦公室。從柱間往外望，看到的是荷李活道。

Third Floor Veranda, Headquarters Block

This photograph was taken outside the officers' mess. It used to be packed with steel file cabinets. It was said that non-police staff would practice taichi here in the morning and during lunch before work.

Behind the round window at the other end of the veranda was the CID office. Hollywood Road can be seen through the columns.

總部大樓二樓

通往總部大樓地下層的樓梯。相中可見十九世紀的半圓窗，樓梯扶手的花紋亦摻有英式傳統建築風格的味道。

地下一層曾經駐有交通意外調查組，港島總區／中區庶務警長室（雜務），中區行動主任辦公室，特別任務隊（黃、賭、毒）及中區交通隊辦公室／香港島交通隊。

First Floor, Headquarters Block

The staircase leads to the ground floor. The semi-circular windows originally built in the 19th century can still be seen, and the stair railings suggest a traditional British architectural style.

Situated on the first floor of the basement were, at different periods, the Accident Investigation Section, Island Headquarters/Central District Barrack Sergeant's office, Central District Operations Officer's office, Special Duties Squad (Prostitution, Gambling and Drug Peddling) as well as the Island Traffic Team/Central District Traffic Team.

總部大樓地下（即荷李活道入口）

不取道樓梯而往左轉，進去就是交通意外組報案室。後來報案室搬往停車場旁的房間，這裏就遷進了九九九報案熱線中心。

1950年代以前，西邊地庫還未分成上下兩層，因此樓底很高，時有警員在這裏打羽毛球，放鬆一下身心。

Ground Floor/Hollywood Front Entrance, Headquarters Block

If one turned to the left instead of going up, one would find the report room of the Accident Investigation Section. After the report room was relocated to the room next to the parking lot, the space became the Regional Command and Control Centre (the 999 Hotline Centre).

Before the basement at the west end was split into two floors in the 1950s, it's high ceiling allowed the police officers to play badminton there for relaxation.

總部大樓二樓天井

天花上有一層通空瓦頂，為了透光，也好讓空氣流通。

相中左邊的位置曾經是廚房，為住在A至D座的外籍警務人員提供西式伙食，煮食的油煙會透過排水位散走。後來廚房改為港島總區及中區庶務警長室，聞説會有庶務警長在這裏煎煮羊扒款待長官，氣味從通風口往上散去，香氣四溢。

First Floor Light Well, Headquarters Block

The light well has an open lattice cover that allows for natural light and ventilation.

A kitchen used to sit on the left of this well to provide foreign officers residing in Dormitory Blocks A to D with western food. Kitchen fumes were expelled through the vents. This space was later repurposed into the office of the Island Headquarters / Central District Barrack Sergeant. It was said that, when the Barrack Sergeant pan-fried mutton chops for his superiors, the aroma rose up along the well, spreading everywhere.

總部大樓二樓地道

行政部外的走廊，一邊是法庭。法庭內有一條秘密通道給法官進入總部大樓，或許就是這裏。

這天花沒有玻璃，疏洞透光，下雨天從這走過會被雨水淋濕。

走廊側邊是中區警署文書房。蚊子多，甚少人會在此逗留。而半圓形的入口能通往大閘後的馬路。

Underpass, First Floor, Headquarters Block

The underpass outside the administration section led to a court.
It might be the secret passage linking the Headquarters block to the Magistrate Court.

As the passage was covered by a mere grating to allow for natural light, one would get wet on a rainy day walking through it.

Beside the passage sat a record room which was more frequented by mosquitoes than humans. The arched exit led through the metal gate to the road from the gate.

營房大樓

建築物東翼是大館，西翼是衝鋒隊，東邊二樓是男更衣室；三樓則是女更衣室。東翼下方是報案室，報案室後是監房，旁邊是槍房，相中西翼還有另一個槍房。

地下位置是中區運輸組，以前設有地下油缸，由當年人稱「油長」的入油員為警車入油。曾經，警車只能在三個地方入油：大館、灣仔和銅鑼灣。後期因發現廿四小時當值需要太多人手，所以改制，讓警車可以在外邊的加油站入油。這是油站封起來其中一個流傳的原因。另一個傳聞是指1980年代有油長不幸地從油車上掉下死亡，後改為由司機自行入油，再加上地下油缸亦因安全理由停用，是故至1990年代，以混凝土封起入油設備。

Barrack Block

Constables occupied the east wing and the Emergency Unit the west wing. Inside the Barrack Block, female changing rooms were at the west end of the second floor, male ones one floor below, and report rooms on the ground floor. Behind the report rooms was the detention room and next to it an armoury. Another armoury was at the west wing.

On the ground floor was the Central District Transport office, equipped with an underground fuel tank for attendants (nicknamed in Cantonese the " oil chief ") to refuel police vehicles. For a while, all polices cars could only be refuelled here, in Wanchai and in Causeway Bay. However, the internal gas stations were closed later, allowing all police cars to refuel at external gas stations. One theory claims that it was to save the expenses of 24-hour service. Another says that after an " oil chief " fell off a tanker to his death in the 1980s, self-service was adopted but eventually abandoned. The petrol station was finally walled in with concrete in the 1990's.

營房大樓

這照片是從B座二樓陽台拍攝的營房大樓。因為四周高樓大廈的阻擋，太陽無法直接投落大樓，照片中投落到大樓的陽光，是從周邊大樓玻璃幕牆的反射而來。而照片裏的大樹，已被砍掉。

十一月天的午後，此情此景，難以復再。

Barrack Block

The Barrack Block seen from the second floor balcony of Dormitory Block B. Encompassed by high-rises, the Barrack Block receives little direct sunshine. The light captured in the picture is reflected from glass curtain walls of neighbouring buildings. The tree in the picture has now been removed.

The atmosphere of this scene, taken in a November afternoon, will be lost forever.

營房大樓

相中右邊的天橋是通往衛生樓的主要通道。衛生樓其實是警員洗澡的地方，在衝鋒隊未有女警時，男警人人只穿拖鞋短褲就走過去，後來有了女警，而且附近居民也有所微言，所以此情此景就從此不再。

大樓頂樓有剪髮服務。當時警員頭髮的長度有嚴格規定，髮側不可過耳，髮尾不可過領。高層警司則常要求理髮師到他們的辦公室內替他們理髮。

The Barrack Block

The footbridges on the right provided primary access to the Sanitary Block, housing the bathroom of the police officers. Male officers once walked around in sandals and shorts, until the recruitment of female officers and complaints received from nearby residents prompted them to be more modest.

Barbers on the top floor kept their hair the regulation length, above the ears on the sides and above the collar at the back. Senior officers often requested to be served in their own offices.

衛生樓

在警隊任職的曾經大部分都是男性，可以想像，當愈來愈多女性擔任警員和文職人員後，雖然有專屬女性的衛生設施，但未能滿足需求。照片中原為男性使用的洗手間，在未經任何改動下，倉卒地改為供女性使用。

Sanitary Block

The police force used to be exclusively male. Presumably, there were sanitation facilities for women, but they could not meet the demand after female constables and officers were inducted into the force. This toilet, equipped for men, was hastily designated for use by women, without refitting.

總部大樓（荷李活道入口）

置身於高樓大廈群之中的總部大樓，屋頂仍保持興建時原初的結構，只有如照片中所見，早上七時的陽光才能投落建築物的東邊。

在晨光暗影下的建築物為未婚警察宿舍，後來改為診所。

Hollywood Front Entrance, Headquarters Block

A dwarf among the giants, the Headquarters Block is only graced on its eastern side by the morning sun. This photo was taken at 7 a.m. The original rooftop structure as seen has remained since its construction.

The part in the shade was once the married quarters and later a clinic.

亞畢諾道

圍牆外的彎位，從前曾有一小屋予警署的雜工居住。而建築物外有頂蓋的地方是洗衣房。

洗衣房在戰前已開業，由人稱肥婆的李四妹打理，承包警隊洗衣服務。由於洗衣房設有鍋爐及大型浸池，戰時，日軍把洗衣房改為洗浴場。戰後，洗衣房恢復運作，每天營運12小時，房內設有一排洗衣專用石水盤。每天早上8時，水喉大開，流水不斷，工人用人手搓揉、擦洗衣服，多年不變。警員制服經常滿佈各種污垢、血跡、泥污，而警隊對制服要求甚高，制服既要清潔，又要挺直，制服經洗滌後須上漿，漿好再燙。洗衣工作之繁重，可想而知。

2004年大館關閉，洗衣房結業，李四妹以83歲高齡榮休。

Arbuthnot Road

What is now a roundabout used to be the location of a cottage for general labourers working at the police station. The structure with covers was the laundry run by a woman called Lee Sai Mui, nicknamed Fei Po (literally "the fat woman"). She had served the police since the pre-war time. During the war, the laundry with boilers and a large soaking tub was used by the Japanese military as ofuro. After the war, laundry service resumed and ran for 12 hours a day. Over a row of stone basins and under taps that started running from 8 a.m. each day, the uniforms, often full of dirt, smudges and blood stains, were hand-washed, scrubbed with brushes, starched and ironed thoroughly in order to look clean and well-pressed. Despite the hard work, the practice lasted for years.

營房大樓槍房

上司信任的人才可擔任這裏的職位，可說是一種榮耀。但一個人在這上班其實挺悶，吃飯、去洗手間也得找人暫代，回房時還要交收點數，十分麻煩，所以當值的警員都盡可能不離開槍房。在槍房當值的警員需要早半小時上班，要預先準備好接下一更的警員需要的槍械彈藥。

槍房的工作也頗多，空閒時要「散槍」，為槍枝塗上薄油，以防生銹，下雨天更要抹乾所有槍枝上的水珠水氣，還要給無線電機充電，很是忙碌。

Armoury, Barrack Block

It was an honour to be appointed by one's superior to assume responsibility for the Armoury as it signalled trust. However, the position was in fact rather dull and troublesome. The appointed officer was required to find a substitute officer whenever he needed to leave for meals or the washroom, and to conduct thorough handover and inventory verification upon return. To avoid that, he would stay in as much as possible. In addition, the appointed officer had to report to work half an hour earlier to prepare all arms and ammunition required by the colleagues on the next shift.

The duty officer had numerous duties, including oiling the guns to prevent rusting, wiping them dry on rainy days, and recharging mobile radio batteries.

報案室後槍房領槍處

為了安全，警員槍枝上彈和退彈均需要在指定的地方進行，就在照片中槍房門邊的牆後。那裏的牆身有厚物質，若有意外走火，牆身物質足以把子彈吸着，不致反彈。而且每次上彈退彈，必須在上級在場下，集體進行。

Arms and Ammunition Collection Point behind the Report Room

For safety reasons, loading and unloading were conducted in a designated area behind the wall next to the door of the armoury in the photo. The anti-ballistic lining of the wall would prevent ricochet in the case of an accidental discharge. Every round of loading/unloading was completed in a group and attended by supervisors.

營房大樓二樓西走廊

飯堂外的走道，右邊的房間是休息娛樂室，內裏設有電視、電子遊戲機、彈子機。娛樂室以合作社方式經營，記賬簽數，警員每月交付茶水飲品費（不賣食物）。彈子機每局收費，警員閒時對彈子機「進貢」，收益撥入福利金，以便向警員提供更廉價的茶水飲品。

1990年代初，飯堂空間不夠，會在這裏再加設白枱椅，94、95年再裝上相中兩枝燈和吊扇，看來充滿歐陸風情，是下午茶的好地方。

Western Corridor, First Floor, Barrack Block

The corridor outside the canteen led to a recreation room on the right where officers watched television, played electronic games and the pinball machine. The recreation room was run as a co-op where uses were recorded in a ledger. The police officers paid a monthly beverage fee and for each game on the pinball machine. Income from the pinball machine was used as a welfare fund to provide the police officers with discounted beverages.

When the canteen became overcrowded in the early 1990s, white tables and chairs were added to the corridor to provide seats. With the two floor lamps and the ceiling fan added in 1994–1995, the effect was quite continental, suitable for afternoon tea.

營房大樓由二樓通往三樓梯間

梯級及扶手均為木製。照片上方可見的屋頂維持了原初的結構，保留至今，由於所歷經時，每每會漏水，也為白蟻蛀食，得經常維修。在1997至1998年間，大樓進行大翻新，屋頂亦更換了瓦片，通風且防水。

Stairs between First and Second Floors, Barrack Block

The steps and railings are all made of wood. The rooftop, as seen in the photo, has retained its original structure through the years. It was prone to water seepage and termites, and has undergone repairs time and again. During the major revamp of the Barrack Block in 1997–1998, the roof tiles were replaced to improve ventilation and water-resistance.

營房大樓二樓東走廊

中間是更衣室，兩旁房間為休息室。夏天，更衣室熱，走廊會擺放上長木凳，以便警員穿鞋，擦鞋，也是警員閒來聊天的聚腳地。1970至1980年代，每有節慶，警員會在這裏開派對。

警員回憶當年有情景如此：「那時生活簡單，思想亦較單純，最難忘聖誕節開派對，飲品食物很簡單。我們會邀請外面正經女子參加，有老師、護士。我們一隊警員一起結識女仔，一起交流，很有團隊精神。」

2004年12月17日警隊在大地舉行告別儀式，正式將中區警署交回政府，當時照片中的整個走道站滿警員，見證大館最後一次的鳴金收兵，同時作別在這地方曾經的那些歲月。

Eastern Corridor, First Floor, Barrack Block

In this part of the building were changing rooms with a resting room on the two sides. Long wooden benches were placed on the corridor for police officers to change or polish their shoes and to chit-chat when the changing rooms heated up in the summer. Parties were also held here at festive times in the 1970s and 1980s.

"Life and expectations were simpler in the old days. The Christmas parties were memorable, although food and drink were basic. We would invite proper ladies like teachers and nurses to join our celebration. The whole team made friends with the girls together. We had a strong team spirit," said a police officer.

On December 17, 2004, a beating retreat ceremony was held on the Parade Ground to mark the official decommissioning of the Central Police Station Compound. Photos taken on the day show the corridor fully packed with police officers to witness the Big Station's very last beating retreat, and to bid farewell to the previous time spent at this place.

營房大樓二樓更衣室

照片中門開光照，感覺寬敞開揚，很難想像當時一隊人只獲分配一間更衣室，衝鋒隊60多人一隊，機動部隊40多人。室內有儲物櫃、木凳，房間兩旁有床鋪。

在特別情況，如「六七暴動」又或是颱風襲港期間，警員須24小時在大館候命，住在離島的警員擔心客船停航，三號風球時就提早回到大館。由於人太多，休息室的床位不夠，警員睡在更衣室地上或六呎高的儲物櫃頂，都是司空見慣之事，有時候一張地蓆也可倒頭大睡去。

Changing Room, Second Floor, Barrack Block

Looking at the changing room in the photo, spacious and bright with open doors, it was hard to imagine how a whole operation unit could fit into a changing room of such size. The truth is: a Tactical Unit typically contained over 40 members, an Emergency Unit over 60; besides, there were lockers, wooden benches and beds on both sides.

On adverse occasions, such as the 1967 Riots or when typhoon strikes, police officers had to stand by at the Barrack around the clock. Officers living far away on outlying islands would report to work during typhoon signal No 3 to avoid suspension of ferry service. With only a few beds to share, it was not unusual for the officers to sleep on the floor, on rollout mats or even on top of the 6-foot-tall lockers.

營房大樓二樓東走廊

更衣室外掛了很多鏡子，幾乎每次的轉身回眸，總能看到自己的身影。

警員上班時換上制服，下班時穿回便服，但不論穿着制服抑或便服，警員必須舉止良好，衣着整潔。1970年代，警員還需在大地列隊，由上司檢查「軍容」。

警員在更衣後，會整理自己儀容，檢查制服有沒有達到穿着要求。照片中的鏡子就是為了這個目的而設置。如果該更衣室有較多的使用者，相對地，鏡子的數目也會有所增加。

Eastern Corridor, First Floor, Barrack Block

A good number of mirrors hang outside the changing rooms by the corridors. One will see one's own reflection every time one turns around.

The police officers came to the changing rooms to put on their uniforms every day before work, and to change back into their casual wear after. They were required to behave and look clean and tidy in and out of uniform. In the 1970s, all the police officers would queue up on the Parade Ground to be inspected by the senior officers.

The mirrors in and out of the changing rooms then were meant for the police officers to check their appearance before leaving the Barrack Block. The more people a changing room held, the more mirrors it had.

營房大樓二樓東走廊

休息室，方便值夜警員下班後能安靜休息，也讓「追更」警員在轉更時可略作小休。有時候警員早上七時下班，下午四時又得上班。

「好像我這類有家室的人怎會在這裏睡，那些和老婆吵架的或許會在這裏睡。」警員回憶起這房間時説着。

事實上，真的沒有太多警員會選擇在這裏睡覺，一來不知道前後有誰剛睡過，擔心衛生問題，也聞説曾經有木蝨的出現，睡覺的要有睡袋。而且房間冷氣不是一開始就有、是後期才安裝的，之前就只有發出「呃呃」聲的吊扇，並不是一個能讓人安心入睡的環境。

Eastern Corridor, First Floor, Barrack Block

These sleeping rooms allowed officers on night shifts to rest. Officers having back-to-back shifts might nap in these rooms as well.

"Married colleagues like me wouldn't stay here, but those who had just quarreled with their wives might do," commented an officer.

Indeed, very few officers preferred to sleep here. Not knowing who slept there before them, they were concerned about hygiene. Fleas were said to be once present in the rooms, and one would need to bring one's own sleeping bag. The ceiling fans also made disturbing noises until they were replaced by air-conditioners.

車長休息室

休息室位於營房的東隅,有行人通道與裁判司署相連。休息室經常有鬧鬼的傳說。有位車長就在這裏午睡時有過兩次鬼壓床的經驗。這或許就是在此供奉一尊關帝像的原因。

Drivers' Lounge

The lounge is located at the eastern-most side of the Barrack Block, connected to the Central Magistracy via a pedestrian bridge. There were talks of it being haunted. In fact, a driver was harassed by ghosts during his nap, twice. This probably explains why there was a statue of Guangung in the lounge.

營房大樓地下

車長調度室內，這個位置是供奉土地公。

關公也有在警署不同地方供奉。曾經，警署供奉了一座大關公，還有盞日夜長開的長明燈，誠心的警員每天上班也會燒香敬拜。

地板由花崗石組成，牆後門外則是予高級警務人員使用的停車場。

Ground Floor, Barrack Block

This shrine in the vehicle dispatch centre is dedicated to the tudi gong (God of the Land).

Meanwhile, several shrines were set up for Guangong at different spots in the police station in the past, with a votary lamp shining continuously placed at the main one. Devoted police officers would offer joss sticks and pay tribute to Guangong daily.

The floor was built from granite. A parking lot for senior officers sat outside this room.

營房大樓東翼地下（報案室後面）

羈留室。設備較簡陋，保安也並非很完善，故只作臨時扣押疑犯之用。若要通宵羈留，得將疑犯押往有標準羈留室的海旁警署。

在一般情況下，扣留疑犯不可超過48小時，如調查需要扣留疑犯更長的時間，亦應在48小時內正式起訴疑犯，或把疑犯送往法庭過堂。

為了防止疑犯自殺，在羈留室內是完全沒有繩索的。疑犯不准穿襪，也沒有毛毯。女性疑犯因衣內不可穿戴胸圍，以免胸圍鐵線成為自殺工具。就連廁所沖水的裝置亦設置在外面，免得疑犯接觸手拉線。因此每當疑犯如廁後，得要警員協助在羈留室外拉動沖水系統。

Ground Floor, East Wing, Barrack Block (Behind the Report Rooms)

This was a sparsely furnished detention cell with laxer security for temporary holding of suspects. For overnight detention, suspects would be brought to a standard detention room at the Water Front Police Station.

Under normal conditions, a suspect could not be detained for over 48 hours. If further detention was required for investigation, an officer must issue a charge sheet and officially charge the suspect, or bring the suspect before a magistrate.

To prevent suicidal attempts, detention cells were free of ropes/wires and wool blankets. Socks were removed from all suspects and brassieres from female suspects to avoid them using the wires inside. Even the chain of the flush was placed outside the cell, and a suspect would require help from police officers to flush the toilet after each use.

營房大樓二樓飯堂

「高級警務人員於紅屋餐廳吃西餐，有專廚款待，一般警員則在飯堂吃中式飯餸。警員平常只得一小時吃飯，只求吃飽，也不會太在意餸菜是否美味。」一位警員説及從前的情況。

飯堂一直以外判方式經營，有一段時間由政府提供特惠水電煤，免租金。飯堂內有大大小小的圓枱，供應的都是碟頭飯，像一般茶餐廳，味道還可以，價錢較外邊的便宜，入境處、懲教處職員亦間有光顧。「當時飯堂的主事人叫四家姐，平常會穿旗袍塗口紅，她有一個員工叫阿黎。飯堂的食物除了提供給伙計外，還有附近的學生。」

攝影師也曾在這兒吃了幾頓午飯，但質素確實一般，便不再光顧了。

照片中牆上那正方形，空了出來的位置，本是供奉着一座關公，其後請移走了。

Canteen, Second Floor, Barrack Block

"While senior officers enjoyed western cuisine prepared by designated chefs at the Red House, lower-ranking officers had ordinary Chinese food in the canteen. We had only an hour for each meal to fill our stomachs, so we didn't pay much attention to the quality," a police officer recalled.

The canteen was outsourced, police officers ate quick rice dishes like those served at an average cha chaan teng. Despite the mediocre quality, staff from the Immigration Department and Correctional Services also came for budget meals. "The person-in-charge of the canteen at the time was called Sei Gaa Ze (literally "the fourth big sister" in Cantonese). She always wore qipao and lipstick. One of the employees was called Ah Lai. Students from nearby schools also came here."

The photographer had lunch here in the 1980's a few times too. Yet, the food quality failed to keep him.

A shrine for Guangong used to stand in front of the square patch on the opposite wall, but was later relocated.

B座外庭

1960至1970年代，制服清洗收費為港幣5仙至1毫，按月付錢。衣服洗淨後不會用乾衣機焗乾，因電費貴，成本高。於是，洗水房外的晾衣場，經常出現壯觀衣海，綠衣、藍衣隨風搖曳，又彷如起伏有序的浪濤，令過路人印象深刻。若由雲咸街看過去，更是壯觀。

衣服吹乾漿燙好後，會由洗衣房的伙計負責把制服送上大館，每天由早上六時多開始送派制服，轉更時又要到更衣室收取更換下來的制服以作清洗，一天得上上落落十多二十次。警員有零錢時，會打賞給洗衣房伙計。

Courtyard, Block B

In the 1960s–1970s, uniform washing service cost 5–10 cents per piece collected monthly. To save expensive electricity and cut cost, uniforms were sun-dried, not machine-dried. A majestic ocean of green and blue waves could be seen by passers-by, and it was most spectacular when seen from Wyndham Street.

Clean and pressed uniforms were dispatched to the police station starting from 6 a.m. every day and collected from changing rooms between shifts. Police officers would tip laundry staff with their spare change since the poor workers had to go up and down the Barrack up to twenty times a day.

馬廄

1925年，這樓高兩層的建築物在總部大樓外空地的西北面建成，一度曾用作軍械庫。其稱為馬廄，是因為在日治時期，日軍在這裏養馬而得名。

這裏，曾經又是港島區「車頭」，即港島區交通組辦公室；再後來交通意外調查組遷至總部地庫，這裏又成為港島重案、便衣探員寫字樓。這裏也曾是職員及訓練主任和翻譯組的辦公室。

Stable Block

The two-storey Stable Block was constructed at the northwest end of the Parade Ground and was used as an armoury for a while. It got its name during the Japanese occupation when horses were kept here by the Japanese military.

The block was occupied by the Island Traffic Team before it moved to the ground floor of the Headquarters. Afterwards, it was taken up in different periods by plain-clothes officers investigating serious crimes, personnel and training as well as the translation unit.

中區警署建築群

左邊的是中央裁判司署，中間的是懲教署休息室，右邊的是營房大樓。

三幢建於不同時期的相連建築。

Central Police Station Compound

Although the Central Magistracy on the left, the Correctional Services' House of Recess in the middle and the Barrack Block on the right were connected, they were constructed in different years.

C座（左邊）

C座和其一旁的B座一樣，都是外籍督察宿舍，其後改為交通警辦公室。女交通警員和女交通督導員主要負責交通意外、超速駕駛的文書工作，如發告票。男交警則負責執行及管制、指揮交通及在有需要時騎鐵馬追截車輛。照片中見到的B座，正是在翻新期間倒塌的位置。

Block C (left)

Block C was the quarter for foreign inspectors and repurposed into the female officers' quarters and the traffic police office in 1950s. While female traffic police and wardens were mainly responsible for clerical work concerning traffic accidents and speeding, such as issuing penalty tickets, their male colleagues took charge of enforcement and control, on-site traffic control, and, if necessary, pursuit and interception of vehicles by motorcycle. The section of the building beyond the pedestrian walkway on the right collapsed during renovation.

B座（右邊）

B座曾經是外籍督察宿舍。宿舍最初是為外籍高級警務人員提供住房和西式伙食服務。木地板長年打蠟得發亮，餐飲服務直遞房間，水準甚高，可媲美酒店。1950年代開始，外籍高級警務人員遷離，這裏成為女警宿舍。

照片中出現的大樹就是停車場外由於被颱風吹倒，無法扶植而被砍掉的一棵；而B座的部分又在建築群翻新工程期間，意外倒塌。如斯光景，從此不再。

Block B (right)

The two blocks were both quarters for foreign inspectors. The wooden floor was carefully waxed until they shone, and western food would be delivered directly to the inspectors' rooms.
The quality of the room service was comparable to that in hotels. After foreign senior officers moved away in the 1950s, Blocks B were converted into the female officers' quarter.

The leaves and branches showing here belonged to a tree in the parking lot. However, it collapsed during a typhoon and was subsequently cut down after attempts to save it were in vain. The building on the right was Block B, which collapsed during renovation. This scene does not exist any more.

B座二樓走廊

有個流傳的故事是這樣的，一名女警員的室友因情在宿舍自殺。隔天晚上，該名女警員下班後與同事一起在宿舍這走廊打麻將，不為意一個回神，抬起頭，看見本已往生的室友在對面樓間向她招手。

這裏，或許就是當年女警員撞鬼的地方。

Second Floor Corridor, Block B

There is a story about the female quarters. It is said that a female officer killed herself at the dormitory because of relationship problems. On the following evening, her roommate played mahjong with other colleagues on the corridor after work. As the roommate raised her head from the mahjong table, the dead friend was seen at the opposite staircase, beckoning at her.

It is quite probable that they were playing mahjong on this spot.

B座二樓

女警宿舍梯間。從前樓梯旁裝有一台電話,供女警員與親友聯絡,有時急趕接電,在木樓梯上奔跑,梯聲很響。

這裏嚴禁男士進入。

Second Floor, Block B

This staircase led to the female officers' quarters. A telephone was installed beside the staircase for the residents to contact their families. Noisy steps would be heard whenever someone rushed over the steps to take a call.

Men were strictly prohibited in this area.

D座二樓

大館內的診所，警員求診需先向上級報告，到槍房放下槍枝，才可見醫生。

對於當時的駐診醫生，警員們有以下回憶和感想：

「最初駐診醫生被稱神醫，雖是西醫，但他父親是中醫，所以他會在用過聽筒後再用手把脈，醫術了得，後來被調到油麻地診所當院長了。接手的同樣是一位『神醫』，不過卻是神經的『神』，無論是甚麼病他都叫病人別洗澡。只要你答應不洗澡，想怎樣就怎樣。例如病人可以要求不要黑色很難喝的『馬尿』，改要黃色那種味道較易入口的咳水。」

Second Floor, Block D

This was the medical post. Before coming here for medical advices, officers had to inform their supervisors and returned theirs guns to the armoury.

Here is an account of the resident doctors by the officers:

"The first resident doctor was exceptionally good. His father was a traditional Chinese medicine doctor and he himself received Western medical training. He took his patient's pulse after using the stethoscope. He was brilliant and was later promoted to head a clinic in Yau Ma Tei. Unfortunately, his successor was exceptionally bad. He asked all his patients to stop washing themselves, whatever conditions they had. As long as you agreed to that, he would let you do whatever you want. He would even prescribe the yellow cough mixture instead of the black one, which we nicknamed "Horse Piss"."

進往停車場的馬路

對於入口處的三棵大樹，警員們如是說道：

「旁邊三棵樹，中間那棵枯了，2002年時我還看到樹幹裏面有一個靈芝。有一對鸚鵡每天早上10時多就會飛來咬樹。」

「這棵樹很大，樹根常撐裂牆，所以會在牆邊貼滿膠尺，膠尺一斷就知道樹根又移位了，所以這條路越整越窄。」

警署關閉後，2007到2009年間，有好幾次颱風，離報案室最近的那棵樹被風吹倒，多次嘗試把它重新扶植不果後，一連氣把另外兩棵樹也一同砍掉。現在，已再難尋得照片中樹影如疏的烈日午後。

Road Leading to the Parking Lot

There were three big trees by the entrance of the parking lot. Some officers recalled:

"Tree in the middle wilted. In 2002, I saw a lingzhi mushroom in it. And a pair of parrots flew here every day at 10 a.m. to peck at the tree."

"This is a giant tree. Its roots often caused damages to the wall beside it. Plastic stripes were attached to the wall to show us shifting of the roots. That's why the road becomes smaller and smaller."

After the decommissioning of the compound, the tree nearest the Reporting Room collapsed in typhoons between 2007 and 2009. Resuscitation was in vain and it was cut down, together with the other two. The shades in the photo will never be seen again.

荷李活道大閘

警署大閘，門長開，只有在「六七暴動」才曾關上。

這是單程路，斜道上方盡頭有一盞交通燈，由一位警員負責操作，稱為「揸電車」。這名警員需要留意大地那邊有沒有車輛駛出，然後控制交通燈。如果見到高官架車離開，就得立即轉燈，令正從荷李活道上來的車輛往後退，而這樣往往令下面那路經常塞車，故總是被投訴。

交通燈在1976、1977年轉用了感應器，但這感應器並不特別敏感，下雨打風時就常常長亮起紅燈又或是綠燈，到了再後來就在地上裝上膠輪感應。

Main Gate, Hollywoord Road

The main gate was always open at the compound. It was shut only during the 1967 Riots.

A police officer used to control the traffic lights at the end of this one-way slope, colloquially referred to as "driving the tram". As preferences were often given to senior officers driving out of the parking lot, there were complaints about the sudden changes of the lights, forcing vehicles going up the slope to roll backwards, causing congestion on Hollywood Road.

A sensor was fitted to replace the manual work in 1976–1977. However, its low sensitivity caused the lights to remain constantly on red or green, especially in bad weather. Transducers were later installed on the ground to detect wheel pressure.

中 央 裁 判 司 署

CENTRAL MAGISTRACY

亞畢諾道正門

中央裁判司署，於1912年至1914年興建，1915年首次用作司法審理。其地牢可通往中區警署，建築風格沿用希臘古典風格，正面的圓形石柱，散發着宏偉莊嚴的感覺。圓柱下低層正中央的是專讓法官進出的門道。

Main Entrance on Arbuthnot Road, Central Magistracy

Built from 1912 to 1914, the Central Magistracy heard its first trial in 1915. The stone columns in classic Greek designs on the façade contribute to the stately impression of the edifice, which is connected with the Central Police Station on the basement level. The door at the centre of the pedestal beneath the columns was restricted to judges.

法庭

落地窗旁的位置是記者、媒體工作人員的旁聽區。公眾人士如出席法庭的聆訊過程，會安排坐在牆前面的座位。牆的另一邊，是總部大樓。窗外的庭園有石梯級連接亞畢諾道，那裏後來用作擺放冷氣系統。

照片中央那道白色牆壁前，法官正襟危坐，在其前方是法庭秘書及翻譯的位置。左邊是證人作供的位置，而法庭中間是檢控官與辯方代表律師的位置。白牆後面是荷李活道。

Courtroom

The media and press sat in on a trial beside the French windows while the public had access to the seats in front of the wall, behind which stands the Central Police Headquarters Block. The courtyard behind the windows has a stone staircase that leads to Arbuthnot Road. The open space is now occupied by a number of compressor units of the air-conditioning system.

The judge sat and presided over a trial in front of the white wall at the centre of the photograph. Immediately in front of the judge sat a stenographer and an interpreter. Witnesses took the stand on the left side of the courtroom while the prosecutor and the defence lawyer sat in the central area. Behind the white wall lies Hollywood Road.

法官辦公室

照片的左下方是壁爐的一角。從前的香港，冬天的時候，氣溫下降至攝氏一、兩度可說是平常事。在暖風機還未出現的日子，要在室內取暖，壁爐可說是最直接可靠了。

Magistrate's office

We can see an old fashioned fireplace in the photograph. Up to the 1960's, the temperature can drop to 1 or 2 degrees Celsius during winter. Without other heating arrangements, a fireplace was still the traditionally preferred way to maintain a comfortable temperature.

法庭旁的辦公室

建築物內空空如也，人去物移，唯關帝依舊在其受供奉的位置，煥發英姿。這裏曾經有一段時間是員佐級辦事處，這座關帝許是當時留下的，大概因未知道供請安座時用了甚麼儀式，故未敢輕易將之請移。

Office near the Courtroom

A statue of Guangong continues to stand tall, watching over the empty space which was once an office of the police of rank and file and where he received daily tribute. The statue has not been relocated likely because no one knows what rituals to conduct so as to agree with those employed to consecrate the statue.

中央裁判司署側門，面向域多利監獄的入口

外牆上的英國皇家盾形紋徽，是英國皇室的象徵，常出現於香港殖民地時期的建築。在1997年7月1日香港政權移交後，所有本港建築物正門上的英國皇家紋徽全被移去，除了已列作古蹟的建築物為例外。亞畢諾道的入口亦有同樣的紋徽。

Side Entrance of Central Magistracy facing Entrance of Victoria Prison

The rock carving bearing a crown on the lintel is emblematic of the British royal family and appeared on many colonial buildings in Hong Kong. Except those on declared monuments, all the other royal emblems have been removed since the handover of Hong Kong on July 1, 1997. The royal crown can also be found above the door on Arbuthnot Road restricted to the judges.

天橋通道

照片中的天橋是營房大樓連接裁判司署的通道，犯人會從這裏進入法庭受審。門頂半圓形的窗是西式建築常用的風格，木製窗花呈蜘蛛網紋，總叫人想起法網難逃這個詞語。這門特別高，聽說從前馬匹也是從這裏進出。

The Footbridge

The footbridge links the Barrack Block to the Magistracy, allowing defendants to enter the latter for trial. The fanlight above the window is typical of western architecture. The spiderweb-like wooden bars remind one of the Chinese proverb: no escape from the web of law. It is said that the door frame was built to its height to allow passage by horses.

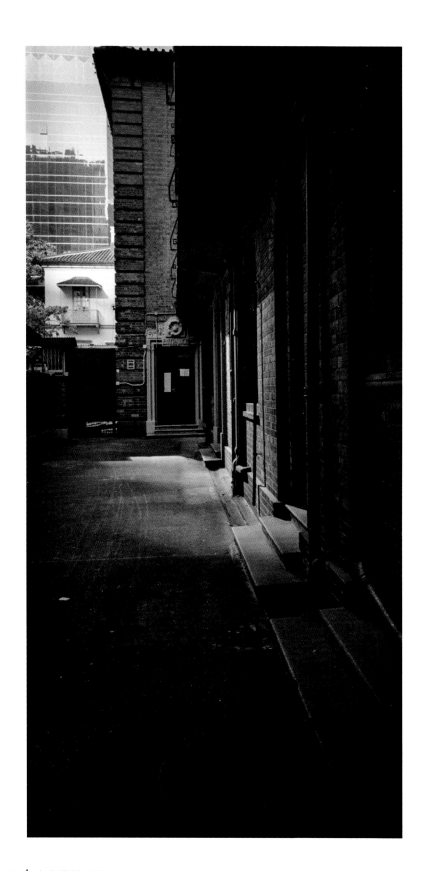

法庭旁走道

這走道在兩建築物間，右邊是法庭，左面前方是獄長樓。在這流連走動的多數是於法庭旁聽審訊的人士。一旁的是文職人員工作的地方，再往裏走，共有四個法庭，可同時審理不同的案件。

The Passage Next to the Courtroom

This passage lies between the judicial courts on the right and a common room of the correctional officers on the left. This was where observers received some sunshine during hearing of court cases. Clerical offices stand between it and the four courtrooms behind which allowed multiple cases to be heard at the same time.

獄長樓入口

石階台是獄長樓的入口，但門已填封，出入得使用側門。此樓建於十九世紀中，共三層，二樓有陽台，曾是懲教署辦公室和宿舍。叢竹生長處，往左轉進去，是庭園。而後面的建築物就是域多利監獄D倉。

Entrance to Superintendent's House

The Superintendent's House sits on top of these stone steps. Its entrance facing the Central Magistracy is now barred leaving the side door for entry. This 3-storey building was built during mid 19th century and was used to be the office of Correctional Services. To the left of the bush is a courtyard. The building behind the bush is D Hall of the Victoria Prison.

獄長樓

通往俱樂部的走道，左邊牆上的光影，是右邊牆洞孔外微弱的燈光所透射出來的。

Ground Floor, Common Room of Correctional Officers

This corridor leads to the correctional officers' club. Faint light behind the wall on the right of the corridor casts patterns on the opposite wall.

獄長樓地下

推門而進的是懲教人員俱樂部。位於樓房的後方。

Ground Floor, Common Room of Correctional Officers

A door at the rear of the building opens onto the correctional officers' club.

裁判司署二樓

在裁判司署撤走後，建築物成為了便衣探員的辦公室。梯間轉角入口的這裏是其中一個辦公室。門旁的信箱寫着HKI AUX HQ，為香港島輔警總部（Hong Kong Island Auxiliary Headquarters）。

First Floor, Central Magistracy

The building was repurposed into an office for the plainclothes officers after the Magistracy moved out. This entry at the turn of the stairs leads to one of the offices. The mailbox beside the entry reads "HKI AUX HQ"- short for "Hong Kong Island Auxiliary Headquarters".

懲教人員休息室

擠放着雙層床。這裏是懲教人員午睡，或是當夜班時小憩的地方。

Common Room of Correctional Officers

Correctional officers probably took naps here in the bunk beds during lunch or night shift breaks.

亞畢諾道贊善里交界

轉角處二樓有兩個長方型窗戶的是紫荊樓，原為更樓，後於1984年改為女囚犯中途宿舍以及單身懲教人員宿舍。後來因安全問題，搬走了。宿舍後的建築物是於同期（1858年）建成的域多利監獄D倉。

Intersection of Arbuthnot Road and Chancery Lane

The structure at the bend of the street with two rectangular windows on the second floor was the Bauhinia House. It was the Watch Tower in 1860s. At the time of 1984, it was used as the half-way house for female prisoners and later the quarters for unmarried correctional officers. The quarters were later relocated due to safety concerns. D Hall of the Victoria Prison can be seen behind the building.

亞畢諾道入口

予公眾進出。特別的圓形拱門設計，裝上鐵閘而非實門。

Public Entrance on Arbuthnot Road

The public accessed the Magistracy through this arched metal gate on Arbuthnot Road.

域 多 利 監 獄

VICTORIA PRISON

D倉外的空地

每天早上及傍晚時份，所有囚犯都要集合到這大空地，四人一排蹲在地上，懲教人員會點算人數。每天最少點數兩次，有時發生特別事件會數四次。懲教人員間或會讓囚犯在空地圍着樹走走，有時又會着囚犯做花王，在地上種薯仔和蕃茄。早期懲教人員發糧是用現金的，曾有一段時間就是在這空地發糧，任由囚犯在場圍觀，也無可奈何。

Courtyard Outside D Hall

Every morning and evening, all prisoners were required to squat down 4 in a row in this courtyard. Correctional officers took the attendance at least twice a day, and up to four times on special occasions. Prisoners were allowed to stroll around the trees in the open lot sometimes, or ordered to do gardening work such as planting potatoes and tomatoes. The correction officers received their salary in cash in the early days. For a while, they were paid here, however reluctantly, in full view of the prisoners.

D倉大門入口通往二樓的木樓梯

地上的花崗岩是原建築時的結構，散發着歷史沉甸甸的氣味。鋪成這地板的花崗岩，是從域多利監獄的後山，由客家人開鑿採運而來。

A Wooden Staircase Leading up to the First Floor Beside the Entrance of D Hall

The flooring, now laden with the sense of history, has remained the same since its construction. The granite used to lay the floor was excavated and transferred by the Hakka people from the hill behind the Victoria Prison to the current site.

D倉地下

牆上的石墩，在監獄未通電前，是用來擺放火把、油燈，以作照明用的。看着照片，想像那久遠的年月，黑夜裏，牆頂旁的燈台映着火光，走道上方那排弧形拱樑或許若隱若現，而耳中迴盪的可能只有鐵門關上那一下的鏗鏘。

Ground Floor, D Hall

Before the prison had power supply, it was lit by fire torches and oil lamps placed on the stone sconces on the wall. Looking at the photograph, one drifts into the imagination of a night in the distant past: the flames on the wall sconces flicker, intermittently revealing the row of arches near the ceiling; the cold, metal door closes, sending a loud clank down the corridor.

D倉二樓樓梯

監倉必須經常保持整潔，禁止牆上塗鴉。監倉內好些地方的油漆工作及恆常的修葺均是囚犯在懲教人員的監督下完成。曾有釋囚憶述在囚期間，獄警若發覺囚犯無所事事，就會指派他們去掃油漆，把整面牆掃好漆後，一次又一次重做。另一方面，獄警亦可藉此以向上司顯示其管制囚犯的能力。

The Staircase Between the First and Second Floors of D Hall

To keep the prison clean and tidy, prisoners were assigned to paint over graffiti on the walls and conduct maintenance work regularly under the supervision of correctional officers. Some prisoners recalled that any of them found idling would be made to paint the walls over and over again. It was a way for the officers to demonstrate their supervisory skills to their superiors.

D倉二樓走廊

門後的本是單人房間。1980至1990年代期間，監獄曾成為轉解及遣返越南船民中心，收容越南難民，當時一間單人房就住上四個人。房內沒有廁所，衛生環境差。床上睡一人，三人睡地上。花崗岩的地面，晚上可是異常的冷。曾於獄內工作的神父說，從來沒有想過香港可以如此冰冷。

Corridor, First Floor, D Hall

The space behind the door was once meant for a single prisoner. During the 1980–1990s, the prison became a transit and repatriation centre for the Vietnamese boat people. Four people packed a single room of poor hygiene and without a toilet en suite. With one already occupying the bed, the other three slept on the granite floor, which became freezing at night. A priest who worked in the prison remembered how he had never thought Hong Kong could be that cold.

D倉二樓

房間裏的是一張雙層床，有時會有木蝨。牆上非吸煙區的標示牌用上三種語言，中文，英文及越南文。聽神父説當時住這裏的越南船民對於紋身很在行，能夠用烏絲燈泡和鉛子筆自製工具。

First Floor, D Hall

A bunk bed, which could have been infested with bedbugs, can still be found in the room. The "Smoke-free Area" sign on the wall is printed in three languages, namely Chinese, English and Vietnamese. A priest praised the tattooing techniques of the Vietnamese boat people staying at the centre who could make their own tools out of tungsten light bulbs and ballpoint pens.

D倉二樓

照片中是康樂及活動空間。長長的走道以這門閘分隔，以便管理，這也是保安措施的一種。聞說有精神科病人喜歡跟着地上那白色圓線繞圈走。精神科移到小欖後，這裏亦改為越南船民及非法入境小孩的學校。他們可在這裏玩耍或進行一些群體活動，例如打乒乓球，有較年輕的可打上數小時。

First Floor, D Hall

The long corridor was reserved for recreational activities of the prisoners. It was divided into compartments by metal doors for management and security purposes. It was said that mental patients would walk along the white circle on the floor. After the psychiatric observation unit in the prison was relocated to Siu Lam, this space was converted to a school for the children of the Vietnamese refugees or illegal immigrants. Young children would play games or sports, such as table tennis, for hours.

D倉二樓

走道左邊門進去是洗手間。1980年代這裏收容越南難民。家庭中若有小孩，就會在這裏玩耍。小孩可以活動及嬉戲的地方很有限，就只這裏及外邊庭園一個小小的地方。照片中的兩個圖畫是越南人離開後，內地非法入境者畫上去的。

First Floor, D Hall

The door on the left of the corridor leads to a washroom. In the 1930s, the prison started accommodating Vietnamese refugees. This was one of the two limited areas where children could play, with the other being the small courtyard outside. The two cartoon figures were drawn by illegal immigrants from Mainland China after the Vietnamese refugees left.

D倉二樓

域多利監獄建成於1841年，為中區警署建築群中最早建成的，比起警察總部大樓早了二十多年完工。1990年代初，中央廣場在亞畢諾道開始動工打地樁，建築物不勝其撞擊之餘力，牆身多處出現大幅裂痕。於是，建築物內加建了鐵樑，用以穩定結構。

First Floor, D Hall

Completed in 1841, about 20 years before the Headquarters Block, the Victoria Prison was the first in the Central Police Station compound to be erected. The prison suffered physical damage in the early 1990s due to the piling activities during the construction of The Centrium on Arbuthnot Road. Walls cracked extensively in multiple locations. Metal beams were thus installed to strengthen the structure.

E倉後房

域多利監獄建築群在十九世紀末二十世紀初建成，當時還沒有出現具沖水系統的如廁設施。在監獄倉房內，有兩個桶，一個裝着淨水，另一個裝排泄物。囚犯每天早上得清理倉房內的兩個桶。這是整個監獄內唯一可以接駁到香港排污系統的地方，囚犯每天早上會排隊，逐一清理桶內之物以及更換清水。

Rear Room, E Hall

The Victoria Prison compound was built between the late 19th and early 20th centuries. At the time, automatic flushing systems for toilets had not been invented yet. Therefore, each prison cell was provided with two buckets, one for clean water, the other human waste. The inmates were responsible for cleaning the buckets in their own cells every morning. This photograph shows the only spot in the whole Victoria Prison that was connected to the city's sewage system. The inmates queued up here every morning to discard their waste and to collect clean water.

D倉二樓

牆上的圖畫可能是越南船民畫的。曾在1994年至1996年間經常進出域多利監獄探望越南船民的神父說，當時有不少越南人也是天主教徒。那時監獄牆上有很多塗鴉，有好一些畫得很漂亮。

First Floor, D Hall

A Vietnamese refugee might have made the drawing on the wall. A number of graffiti drawings can be found on the prison walls, some of them of good quality. According to a priest who was a frequent visitor to the Victoria Prison between 1994 and 1996, many of the Vietnamese refugees were Catholics.

D倉三樓

1961年設立了精神科觀察組，用以收容接受精神檢查、觀察或等候法庭報告的囚犯，直到小欖精神病治療中心在1972年啟用而被其取代。後來改為診所，環境特別潔淨，每兩至三個星期更會有牙醫駐診。1980、1990年代，這裏成了「產房」。當時住在這裏的越南難民懷孕，最希望可以到正規醫生產子，但不是每個人也可得償所願。在這裏誕下的孩子可以跟着媽媽，但卻不能出外上學唸書。

Second Floor, D Hall

A psychiatric observation unit was established in 1961 in the prison to accommodate prisoners undergoing psychiatric examinations, observation or awaiting judiciary decisions. Replaced by the Siu Lam Psychiatric Centre in 1972, the space was converted to a general clinic which also provided dental service once every two to three weeks. This area was kept spotless. The space was repurposed again into a delivery room in the 1980s–1990s. Although all the pregnant Vietnamese refugees wished to give birth in a proper hospital, not all saw their hopes come true. Babies born in the centre could stay with their mothers but had no right to go to school.

D倉三樓

鐵窗，鐵閘門，是監獄直接得近於原始的象徵。在監房的牆內，有時可見劃了上去的文字。難以考證是哪種語言，像是印度，又可能是緬甸又或是來自東南亞地區的文字。

Second Floor, D Hall

Window frames and doors made of metal are the most explicit, almost primitive, symbols of the prison. Word carvings can be found on some walls in the prison. It is hard to distinguish the origin of the language but it seemed to belong to India, Cambodia or somewhere in the Southeast Asian region.

D倉三樓

高峰期住了二千多個難民，大部分是越南難民。這本是二人房間，一度同時住進六人。當時的越南難民，一家人睡在一張床上。

Second Floor, D Hall

At its peak, the centre accommodated over 2,000 refugees, largely from Vietnam, with six people packed in a double room. A whole family was required to share one bed.

C倉二樓

英式的建築設計，屋頂有兩層天花，交錯而建，使得兩層之間有空隙，充當排氣口，空氣得以流通，又不至於在雨天時入水。中間的是鐵網，為了防止囚犯墮下而裝上的。這些本來都是單人倉房。但細看鐵門左方那個正方形鐵牌，後來可以放三，四個囚犯的號碼或名字了。

First Floor, C Hall

Built in the English style, the ceiling of the hall is clerestoried to allow ventilation through the crevices while blocking water seepage on rainy days. The metal mesh between the two floors was fitted to prevent prisoners from falling. The cells were built as single cells, but the square-shaped metal frame on each door held up to three to four names in the later days.

E倉地下

這是1915年建成的E倉，採用了典型英式監獄的設計。中間一道鐵樓梯，左右兩邊是倉房，兩邊牆壁頂部有長方形的缺口，用作氣孔。這道長長的鐵樓梯，晚上獄警巡倉時若穿皮鞋，走在梯間會十分吵耳，囚犯投訴得很厲害，有時更會破口大罵，所以大部分獄警在晚上當值時會穿上橡膠底帆布鞋，他們稱之為「一星期鞋」。因為這底子的鞋不耐穿，易磨損，很快要換掉。

Ground Floor, E Hall

Built in 1915, E Hall follows the classical design of English prisons: a metal staircase stands in the middle of the hall with prison cells lining both sides; and rectangular openings near the ceiling allow air circulation. As leather shoes would produce great noises on the long, metal staircase, provoking angry complaints or even curses from the prisoners, most of the officers would slip into their plimsolls when they were on duty. Fragile and quick to wear out, the plimsolls were nicknamed the "one-week shoes".

B倉二樓，獄內的廚房

囚犯負責煮飯，警長負責看守。這類伙頭是從內部挑選的，多是一些刑期短、沒暴力傾向、犯刑時沒持槍或持刀案底的。不是每個囚犯也懂得煮食，雖然負責看守的警長會從旁指導，但煮出來的食物的味道亦多難以下嚥。「有時候煮飯那位連米要洗也不知道，飯煮出來是黃色的；那時每天午飯只吃粥，煮出來的粥又總是黑色的。」一位釋囚回憶道。

Kitchen, First Floor, B Hall

Cooking was done by prisoners under the supervision of a sergeant. Those selected to work in the kitchen were usually short-term serving prisoners with no violent tendencies or records of use of guns or knives. Since not all those selected knew how to cook, their cooking was often quite unpalatable despite guidance from the sergeant. "Sometimes the rice came out yellowish because it was not rinsed. The rice congee we had for everyday lunch often came out black and burnt," a former prisoner recounted.

B倉二樓，飯堂

囚犯一個接一個排隊取飯。負責派飯的伙頭只會看到囚犯的手，看不到他們的樣子，以示公平。但據釋囚說，囚犯為着能有更好的伙食，會私下與伙頭有交易，並以手勢為溝通與識認的暗號。

Canteen, First Floor, B Hall

Prisoners queued up here to collect their meals. To ensure a fair deal for everyone, the prisoner assigned to serve meals could see only the hands of his/her fellows but not their faces through the small opening. Nonetheless, former prisoners said some would use hand signals to ask the server, with whom they had a deal, to give them bigger portions or better food.

從D倉到C倉

照片裏右邊的石階往上走，會到達D倉，左邊往下走會通往C倉。
這是D倉與C倉兩建築間的空地。右邊石牆曾是以前執行死刑（絞
刑）的地點，後來行刑地改到赤柱監獄。

Staircase connecting D and C Halls

The staircase leads up to D Hall and down to C Hall. The wall on the right used to support the gallows. However, the gallows was later moved to the Stanley Prison.

D倉停屍間

若囚犯不幸在獄中身亡，會被移至此處，先作清洗，再進行葬禮。
洗刷屍體時，水從石床中間的坑道中流走。

Morgue, D Hall

The bodies of the inmates who passed away in the prison were brought
here to clean before disposal. The groove at the centre of the stone bed
allowed liquids to drain off during the cleaning process.

E倉地牢

日間囚犯會在這些如鐵籠般的工作間裏車熨衣衫，做木工又或是在小休時看一會電視。到了收容越南船民的時期，因為人數太多，這裏不再是工作間，而是改為住人的地方。船民得自己洗衫，掛起晾乾也是在這裏，所以夏天的時候，潮濕非常。

Basement, E Hall

In the daytime, prisoners did the sewing, ironing, woodwork or watch the television during breaks in these cage-like compartments. With the influxes of the Vietnamese boat people, this area was converted to accommodate the refugees. The space became sultry as the refugees did their laundry and airing here.

E倉地牢

看着照片，可能會聯想到教堂，囚犯或被囚的船民祈禱的地方。有一說法是監獄內每星期會舉行禮拜，吸引很多囚犯參與，因為有糖吃；另一說法卻指監獄內從未有禮拜活動。

Basement, E Hall

The scene brings to mind a church or a place for the prisoners or refugees to pray. Some said church services were held weekly in the prison when sweets were distributed, attracting numerous prisoners to join in; others disputed the presence of such activities.

D倉往E倉的通道

照片中的一棵樹，有一段時間曾圍上了鐵絲網。起因是有囚犯爬了
上樹不肯下來。

Passage between D and E Halls

One of the trees in this photograph was lapped in barbed wires for a
period of time after an inmate refused to climb down from the tree.

始建於1898的F倉

1929重建成兩層高的建築物，後於二戰期間建築物受到破壞，1948年重修，處理政府印刷事務。及後於1956年修葺，並成為監獄的一部份。二戰前樓上曾是一個車衣工場，後來成為大監倉，樓下有一部份是用作監獄的行政辦公室及探訪者接待處。

F Hall (Built in 1898)

F Hall was reconstructed into a two-storey building in 1929 which was damaged during the Second World War. It was then rebuilt in 1948 as a printing press for the government. Before it finally joined the Victoria Prison, the structure received further restoration in 1956. The upper level was first purposed as a sewing workshop and then a large prison, while parts of the lower level housed the prison's administrative office and the visitor reception.

F倉地下

住進監獄的人需要換上一式一樣的囚衣，其原本的那身衣衫就會放在左邊這房間，待可以離開的時候再作更換。右方的廁所沒有裝上門，這是因着保安的理由，以讓獄警可一眼看到內裏的情況。右方門內的鏡子是凸圓鏡，可清楚照見整個房間內的情況。

Ground Floor, F Hall

The inmates were required to wear uniforms during their time behind bars. Their own clothing would be deposited in the room on the left and returned upon discharge. For security reasons, the toilet on the right had no doors so that the guards could keep an eye on the inside through the convex mirror.

F倉二樓

曾經的車衣工場，在1990年代期間，曾住上千多人。一邊是非法入境者，另一邊是越南船民。同一地方，以鐵籠分隔，一邊為睡住之域，一邊為工場之處，從早到晚，就在這空間消磨了。

First Floor, F Hall

In the 1990s, the sewing workshop once accommodated over a thousand prisoners with illegal immigrants in one compartment and Vietnamese refugees in another. With the sleeping area merely a grille from the work area, the prisoners counted the hours in the same space day in, day out.

F倉二樓

囚犯在領取剪刀時需出示號碼布，把剪刀拿走後原位會換掛上號碼布。囚犯工作完畢後交還剪刀，就可取回號碼布。工作人員對這些剪刀非常着緊，如果有一把剪刀不見了，整個倉的囚犯也不能離開，一定得找回方休。因為剪刀可以變成傷人的工具。在處理剪刀時，囚犯亦會非常謹慎，不會隨便亂放，而且一定放近身邊。每一架衣車都有一個抽屜可放剪刀。

First Floor, F Hall

Before the inmates received their scissors for work, they were required to produce their number bibs, which would be hung in place of the scissors. They must return the scissors after work so to retrieve their bibs. As the scissors could be dangerous weapons, there were measures to prevent possession by the inmates. Each person handled his/her tool cautiously, kept it close by his/her side or placed it in the drawer beneath his/her sewing machine. Whenever a pair of scissors went missing, none of the inmates would be allowed to leave the workshop until the missing scissors were recovered.

F倉地下後座

到獄中探望在囚親友的訪客是不可以直接觸囚犯，即使面對面，也得隔着玻璃，通過傳話筒溝通，而全程對話亦會被錄音。電話傳聲大有所失，對話的聲量也需比平常提高。但這樣一來，相鄰的那位又會被騷擾，於是大家一起越來越大聲。這樣，整個探望室也吵耳非常，幾乎是聽不見對方的説話。

Rear Ground Floor, F Hall

Families and friends visiting were prohibited from coming into direct contact with the inmates. Face-to-face conversation was conducted through a glass panel and a recorded intercom system. The speakers often had to raise their voice so to make up for the volume loss over the intercom. As one spoke up, so did the neighbours. Eventually, nearly all were drowned out by the cacophony.

F倉的指模房

犯人被送進監獄時，要先在這裏登記、換上獄衣、拿過號碼布、四張氈一張蓆和其他一些生活用品，就離開這房間，正式開始其牢獄生涯。左邊牆柱上的橫間牌子，就是拍攝囚犯照時的背景，牌子上可清楚見到「攝影區」三個字。

The Fingerprint Room of F Hall

New inmates were brought here upon admission for registration, to change into their uniforms and to pick up, for each person, a number bib, four blankets, a rolling mat and other daily necessities. Stepping out of this room, they officially entered his/her term of imprisonment. The board with horizontal lines on the pillar on the left served as the background of mug shots. The Chinese equivalent of "Photography Zone" can still be seen printed at the top of the board.

B倉旁

中央的部分是囚犯等待診症，或是輪候驗身的地方，左邊則是醫生房。

B Hall

Inmates queued up in the central area in the photograph for medical diagnosis or health checks in the doctor's practice on the left.

從入境處辦公室看監獄

左邊的是A倉，右邊是C倉。這本是由警署通往監獄的通道，後因為越南難民和非法入境者搬進監獄，於是成了入境處的臨時辦公室。

View of Prison from Immigration Office

This passage, between A Hall on the left and C Hall on the right, used to link the prison and the police office together. It was later converted into a provisional office of the Immigration Office after the Vietnamese refugees and illegal immigrants were relocated into the prison.

入境處辦公室閘口

域多利監獄大部分建築原材料都是從英國運來，照片上的地蓋即是一例。地蓋上鑄上DOULTON字樣，是十九世紀時製造瓷器和去水管的公司，後來經英國皇室發牌改名為Royal Doulton，現在在英國是一間有名的瓷器公司。當時就連警察制服的鈕扣，也是從英國運來的。左邊的抽屜是供進入監獄範圍工作的人暫存手提電話。

Entrance Gate, Immigration Office

All materials used to build the Victoria Prison were imported from the U.K., including the manhole cover in the photograph. The name "Doulton" appearing on it belonged to a company which started out manufacturing stoneware and drainage pipes in the 19th century. When it was granted the royal warran, it became Royal Doulton, and is now a well known manufacturer of fine china. In fact, at that time, even the buttons on police uniforms were sourced from England. And the drawers on the left were for storing mobile phones of people who came to work in the prison.

監獄出口

門是藍色的，是囚犯在刑期屆滿後，離開監獄的出口。有說道監獄生涯，由黃色門開始，藍色門結束。囚犯相信離開時候絕不能回望，否則會再受牢獄之苦。

Exit of Prison

The door in blue was the exit prisoners took upon discharge. A saying went: prison life begins at the yellow door and ends at the blue one. It was a common belief among prisoners that they should never look back while leaving the prison, otherwise they will come back again.

贊善里

這是在贊善里的監獄圍牆，由花崗岩石砌成。牆身曾經加高，因為以前囚犯可以常常收到由牆外拋進監獄的「禮物」。在1980年代期間曾有一次逃獄事件，那個倒霉的犯人爬上圍牆，勇身跳下，就只落得跌斷腿的下場，轉眼又被捉回去了。攝影師住在監獄附近的一棟住宅大廈，可以俯瞰監獄。

Chancery Lane

The granite wall of the Prison borders in Chancery Lane. The height has been augmented because the convicts used to receive "gifts" thrown over the wall. In the 1980s when the photographer lived in an apartment overlooking the Prison, there was an escape attempt. The unlucky prisoner scaled the wall and jumped down, only to break his legs and was easily captured.

參考資料 REFERENCE

書目 Publication

何耀生，《集體回憶之中區警署：百年警署的故事》，香港：明報，2005年。

何明新，《大館 —— 中央警署 跨世紀檔案》，香港：中華書局，2016年。

何家騏、朱耀光、何明新，《謹以至誠 —— 香港警察歷史影像》，香港：商務印書館，2014年。

薛求理，《城境 —— 香港建築1946–2011》，香港：商務印書館，2014年。

網頁 Website

古物古蹟辦事處網頁 Website of Antiquities and Monuments Office: www.amo.gov.hk

香港記憶 Hong Kong Memory: www.hkmemory.hk/

香港發展局文物保育網站 Development Bureau heritage conservation website: www.heritage.gov.hk

大館網頁 Website of Tai Kwun: www.taikwun.hk/

香港政府新聞網 News. Gov. HK: www.news.gov.hk

鳴謝 ACKNOWLEDGEMENTS

盧秀麗 **Fione Lo**

黃淑霞 **Beatrice Wong**

何仲詩 **Joyce Ho**

劉振明 **Lau Chun Ming**

劉達強 **Lau Tat Keung**

趙成球 **Ben Chiu**

曹永偕 **Cho Wing Kai**

丘瑞恆 **Yau Sui Hang**

陸海浩 **Luk Hoi Ho**

陳善慶 **Chan Sin Hing**

畢庶雄 **But Shu Hung**

陸金成 **Luk Kam Sing**

徐德有 **Chui Tak Yau**

黃俐燕 **Bryony Hardy Wong**

苗絲敏 **Wendy Miu**

晶姐

畢神父

文錦棠

Stanley Dirkin

Shirley Dirkin

John Rhind

Garth Hydes

Theodora Thunder

Peter and Liz Whiteside

古物古跡辦事處 **Antiquities and Monuments Office of the Leisure and Cultural Services Department**

香港建築中心 **Hong Kong Architecture Centre**

梁家泰　　　攝影 / 文字
Leong Ka Tai　**Photography / Text**

林道群　　　編輯
Lam To Kwan　**Editor**

祝雅妍　　　編輯 / 文字 / 中文翻譯
Phoebe Chuk　**Editorial / Text / Chinese Translation**

陳若瑛　　　設計 / 插圖
Helen Chan　**Design / Illustration**

秦海迪　　　英文翻譯
Heidi Chun　**English Translation**